The 2014 WWE® WrestleMania® annual

Welcome WWE fanatics to the 2014 WWE *WrestleMania* annual. Every page is packed with info, overflowing with things to do, stacked with Superstar stats and Diva details and bursting at the seams with the best matches ever seen. Whether you're a long-term WWE mega fan or are just dipping your toe into the world of sports entertainment, there's loads for you to do and learn to ensure you're the heavyweight king of WWE amongst your buddies! Let's not waste another minute. The bell's ringing, let's get stuck in!

Published 2013. Century Books Ltd.
Unit 1, Upside Station Building Solsbro Road,
Torquay, Devon, UK, TQ26FD

info@centurybooks.co.uk

CONTENTS

£7.99

WRESTLEMANIA®

THE ESSENTIAL FACTS

The worldwide phenomenon, The Showcase of Immortals, whatever you call *WrestleMania*, no one can doubt it's the ultimate event in sports entertainment! Over the course of the 29 years, it's treated us to some of the most memorable match-ups in history – here's just a few of the facts about sports' biggest night that you should know!

There have been 109 title matches in *WrestleMania* history. In that time, 53 percent of defending champions have successfully retained their title on The Grandest Stage of Them All.

The rule that states that WWE titles cannot change hands by count-out or disqualification means that five different titleholders – Shawn Michaels, Greg "The Hammer" Valentine, The Honky Tonk Man, Mr. Perfect and Jeff Jarrett – have retained their championships at *WrestleMania* despite losing their matches.

UNDERTAKER HAS APPEARED AT MORE CONSECUTIVE *WRESTLEMANIAS* THAN ANYONE ELSE, AN INCREDIBLE 13. THE DEADMAN ALSO HOLDS THE RECORD FOR MOST WINS, 21 AND COUNTING!

No Superstar has appeared at every *WrestleMania*. In fact, only one person can claim that esteemed honour. Ring announcer Howard Finkel has handled the mic at every show since 1985!

HULK HOGAN'S MATCH WITH KING KONG BUNDY IS THE ONLY STEEL CAGE MATCH IN *WRESTLEMANIA* HISTORY.

Christian is the only Superstar to fight in championship bouts in three consecutive *WrestleManias*. He won the Tag Team Title in a three-way Ladder Match at *WrestleMania 2000*, scored tag team glory again in a Tables, Ladders and Chairs Match at *WrestleMania X-Seven* but wound up on the losing end in his European Championship Match against Diamond Dallas Page at *WrestleMania X8*.

WrestleMania XIV – the first time WWE fanatics heard The Rock's classic catchphrase, 'If you smell what The Rock is cooking'!

Over the years, Shawn Michaels has spent more time than any other in the ring at *WrestleMania*. In all, an unbelievable 378 minutes!

TRIPLE H AND JOHN CENA HOLD THE RECORD FOR MOST CHAMPIONSHIP MATCHES AT THE GREATEST SHOW OF THEM ALL. BOTH HAVE FOUGHT FOR THE GOLD EIGHT TIMES.

Brock Lesnar is the only man in WWE History to make his *WrestleMania* debut in a main event Championship match.

Hulk Hogan is the only man to hold the title from *WrestleMania* to *WrestleMania* without losing it.

Macho Man Randy Savage holds the title for the having the most wins at a single

WrestleMania. He won four matches in one night at *WrestleMania IV*.

Triple H has the dubious title of having the most losses at *WrestleMania* with nine.

Only one match in *WrestleMania* has ended in a time-limit draw. When Jake "The Snake" Roberts and Ravishing Rick Rude met in a tournament match at *WrestleMania IV*, a 15-minute time limit was reached. But despite the bell ringing on their match, the fighting didn't stop as the two Superstars fought long into the night!

THERE HAVE BEEN 27 NEW WORLD TITLE HOLDERS CROWNED IN THE 29 EDITIONS OF *WRESTLEMANIA* – *RAW* AND *SMACKDOWN* HAVE NEEDED NEARLY 1,700 EPISODES TO COMPLETE THE SAME FEAT!

NAME: RYBACK
FROM: SIN CITY
YOU SHOULD KNOW: RYBACK CONTINUES TO DEVELOP HIS FORMIDABLE TALENTS AND SHEER POWER WITH EACH PASSING DAY!

NAME: THE MIZ
FROM: CLEVELAND, OHIO
YOU SHOULD KNOW: IN 2013, THE MIZ STARED IN THE MARINE 3: HOMEFRONT, THE LATEST INSTALLMENT OF WWE STUDIOS' EXPLOSIVE ACTION MOVIE SERIES

NAME: SANTINO MARELLA
FROM: CALABRIA, ITALY
YOU SHOULD KNOW: IF HE'S NOT IN THE RING COMPETING, OR ON THE MIC, HE'LL BE TRUMPETING HIS INVISIBLE BRASS BAND. SANTINO ALWAYS ENTERTAINS!

NAME: CURTIS AXEL
FROM: CHAMPLIN, MINNESOTA
YOU SHOULD KNOW: AXEL IS A THIRD-GENERATION COMPETITOR. HE'S THE GRANDSON OF LARRY THE AXE HENNIG AND THE SON OF MR. PERFECT CURT HENNIG.

PAGE 80 – CROSSED WORDS

PAGE 81 – SUPERSTAR CROSSWORD

"Here comes the champion. The Rock is soaking up the crowd's reaction as he makes his way to the ring. "

"After a back and forth battle, he came out on top the last time they met. Can he prevail against the Cenation again tonight?"

"We don't have long to wait to find out!"

"And that's what it's all about folks, the WWE Championship. What a match we have here!"

"And the action is under way! They tie up and Rock catches Cena in a headlock before being sent into the ropes…"

"…Rock comes blasting out with a huge clothesline on the Cenation…"

"…Somehow Cena takes the upper hand and drops an almighty body slam on the champion!"

"This is nip and tuck wrestling, it's impossible to predict how this match is going to go!"

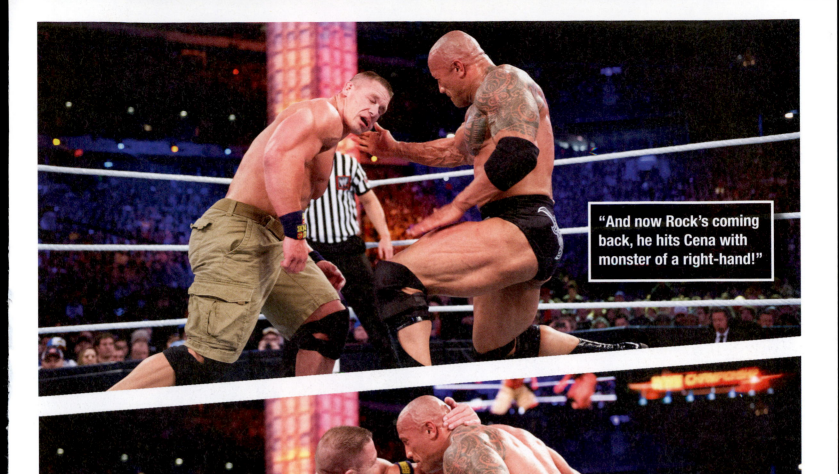

"And now Rock's coming back, he hits Cena with monster of a right-hand!"

"And Cena returns the favour. He's dropped the People's Champion with ferocious right of his own…"

"…Cena goes for the cover but the Rock kicks out at two. Something tells me there's a long way yet to go in this fight."

"Cena gets back to work and locks in a deep headlock on The Rock. He's trying to make him tap out…"

"…But the Rock's too much of a veteran to get caught out like that and reverses the hold and catches Cena in a headlock…"

"…And he takes Cena down to the canvas and ties him up in a Sharpshooter. This is incredible action, surely the Cenation will be forced to tap soon!"

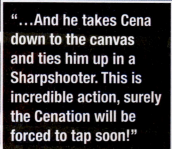

"Everything Rock is throwing at Cena, John is taking! What's it gonna take to beat the Cenation tonight?"

"Rock gives up the hold and instead decides to go for something that will give him the pin. He sends Cena back to the mat with a beautiful hip toss…"

"Rock drops a huge People's Elbow. But, Cena kicks out at two! How is he finding the strength to keep getting up? No stop in the action now as the two titans tangle again…"

"…Rock bounces off the ropes and goes for a high-cross body to bring the action back down to the mat. But Cena has caught him in mid air! Incredible after the pummeling he's just taken."

"From the high cross body catch, Cena uses every last drop of strength he has to hoist Rock onto his shoulders…"

"…and drops him in an incredible Attitude Adjustment! I can't believe what we've just seen!"

"Cena goes for the cover… One, two, three!"

"It's official – John Cena is the new WWE Champion!"

"After going at it for 25 minutes inside the ring, that was one of the most back and forth battles ever witnessed inside the WWE ring."

"Cena's just answered the question of where he got his strength to keep going in that match – the incredible WWE fans!"

"How about this for sportsmanship folks. The Rock presents John Cena with the title, salutes him and raises the new Champ's arm in the air. What an incredible end to an unbelievable match-up. Only in the WWE folks!"

ANSWERS

SO, HOW DID YOU DO?!

PAGE 26 – THE BIG WWE QUIZ – PART ONE

1. Zeb Colter
2. The Shield
3. John Cena
4. Preston
5. Big Show
6. Mr. Perfect Curt Hennig
7. Primo
8. He would be forced to retire
9. 703 lbs
10. Sin Cara, by just one inch!
11. The Million Dollar title
12. Santino Marella's cobra
13. The Royal Rumble Match
14. They couldn't pronounce his name

PAGE 28 – NAME THE SIGNATURE MOVE

1. The Great Khali – Punjabi plunge
2. Wade Barrett – Bull Hammer
3. Sheamus – Brogue Kick
4. Ryback – Shell shocked
5. R-Truth – The Lie Detector
6. The Miz – Skull-Crushing Finale

PAGE 30 – WRESTLE WITH THE DIFFERENCES

PAGE 44 – SWITCHED UP SUPERSTARS

THE ULTIMATE HIGH FLYER

Head – Sin Cara
Arms – Chris Jericho
Torso – Rey Mysterio
Legs & Boots – Kofi Kingston

THE POWERHOUSE

Head – Mark Henry
Torso & Arms – Triple H
Legs – Ryback
Boots – Brock Lesnar

PAGE 48 – IT STARTED WITH A FIST

1 – A, 2 – C, 3 – B, 4 – B,
5 – Trick question! A, B and C all happened in build-up to Punk and Undertaker's *WrestleMania* war!

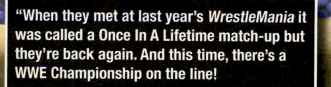

"When they met at last year's *WrestleMania* it was called a Once In A Lifetime match-up but they're back again. And this time, there's a WWE Championship on the line!"

"Wow, John Cena looks ready for action, he's sprinting to the ring so he can get this thing started!"

"I've got goosebumps for this fight already folks! Fans across the world love John Cena, can he use their energy and support to score the WWE gold this evening?"

SMACK DOWN

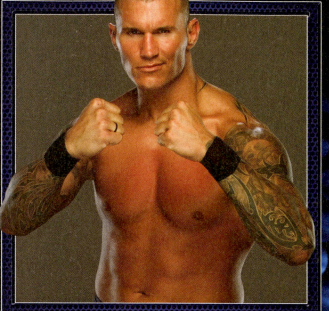

NAME: RANDY ORTON
FROM: ST. LOUIS, MISSOURI
YOU SHOULD KNOW: DESCENDED FROM A WRESTLING FAMILY, AN EARLY MEMORY IS REPAIRING A BANISTER THAT ANDRE THE GIANT HAD LEANED ON!

NAME: ANTONIO CESARO
FROM: LUCERNE, SWITZERLAND
YOU SHOULD KNOW: THIS SWISS-BORN SUPERSTAR IS UNABASHEDLY PROUD OF HIS ROOTS, AND IS QUICK TO REMIND OTHERS OF HIS LUCERNE HOMETOWN.

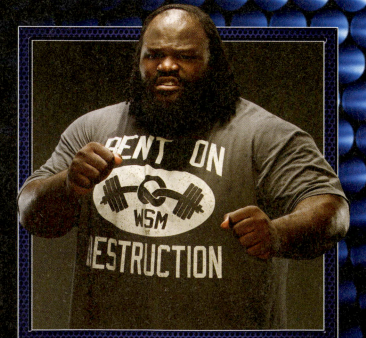

NAME: MARK HENRY
FROM: SILSBEE, TEXAS
YOU SHOULD KNOW: HENRY'S AN OLYMPIAN! HE WENT TO THE 1992 OLYMPICS IN BARCELONA, WHERE HE COMPETED IN WEIGHTLIFTING.

NAME: SHEAMUS
FROM: DUBLIN, IRELAND
YOU SHOULD KNOW: BEFORE HITTING THE BIG TIME IN WWE, SHEAMUS WORKED AS A BODYGUARD FOR IRISH ROCK LEGENDS U2!

THE SUPERSTARS

GET TO KNOW YOUR FAVOURITE RAW SUPERSTARS

NAME: PAUL HEYMAN
FROM: SCARSDALE, N.Y.
YOU SHOULD KNOW: BY AGE 11, HE WAS RUNNING A MAIL ORDER BUSINESS SELLING CELEBRITY AND SPORTS MEMORABILIA FROM HIS HOME.

NAME: KOFI KINGSTON
FROM: GHANA, WEST AFRICA
YOU SHOULD KNOW: IN APRIL 2013, KINGSTON ENDED ANTONIO CESARO'S EIGHT-MONTH US CHAMPIONSHIP REIGN. BUT, HE LOST A DREADLOCK IN THE PROCESS.

NAME: ZEB COLTER
FROM: NASHVILLE, TENN
YOU SHOULD KNOW: A NO-NONSENSE MANAGER NOW, COLTER USED TO WRESTLE HIMSELF. HIS RING NAME WAS DUTCH MANTEL.

NAME: ZACK RYDER
FROM: LONG ISLAND, NEW YORK
YOU SHOULD KNOW: A 21ST CENTURY SUPERSTAR, RYDER USED THE INTERNET AND SOCIAL MEDIA TO CREATE HIS SHOT AT THE WWE BIG TIME.

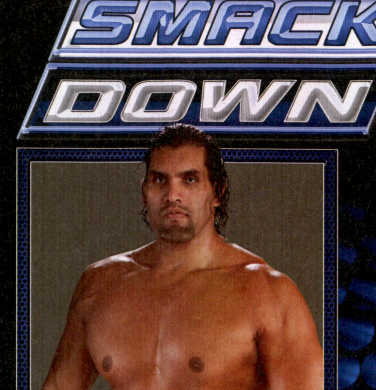

NAME: THE GREAT KHALI
FROM: INDIA
YOU SHOULD KNOW: FROM BOLLYWOOD TO HOLLYWOOD. HE'S HAD STARRING TURNS IN FILMS INCLUDING THE LONGEST YARD, GET SMART AND MACGRUBER.

NAME: SIN CARA
FROM: MEXICO CITY, MEXICO
YOU SHOULD KNOW: COMES FROM A FAMILY WITH WRESTLING IN THE BLOOD. HIS FATHER, THREE BROTHERS AND COUSIN ARE PART OF A WRESTLING LEGACY.

NAME: DARREN YOUNG
FROM: MIAMI, FLORIDA
YOU SHOULD KNOW: YOUNG MIGHT BE EXAGGERATING WHEN HE CALLS HIMSELF MR. NO DAYS OFF, BUT ONLY JUST. HE'S ONE OF THE BUSIEST SUPERSTARS IN WWE.

NAME: TITUS O'NEIL
FROM: LIVE OAK, FLORIDA
YOU SHOULD KNOW: HE IS A FORMER COLLEGE AND PROFESSIONAL FOOTBALL PLAYER AND PLAYED COLLEGE FOOTBALL FOR THE UNIVERSITY OF FLORIDA.

THE SUPERSTARS

GET TO KNOW YOUR FAVOURITE SMACKDOWN SUPERSTARS

NAME: BIG SHOW
FROM: TAMPA, FLORIDA
YOU SHOULD KNOW: HE'S KNOWN FOR HIS PUNCHING POWER BUT MET HIS MATCH AT *WRESTLEMANIA XXIV* WHEN KNOCKED OUT BY FLOYD "MONEY" MAYWEATHER

NAME: WADE BARRETT
FROM: PRESTON, ENGLAND
YOU SHOULD KNOW: WADE HAS A DEGREE IN MARINE BIOLOGY AND WORKED IN A LAB WHILST TRAINING TO BECOME A SUPERSTAR.

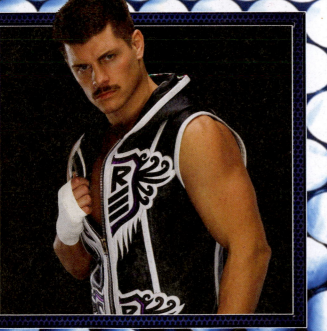

NAME: CODY RHODES
FROM: MARIETTA, GEORGIA
YOU SHOULD KNOW: CODY IS THE SON OF HALL OF FAMER DUSTY RHODES. HE GREW UP WATCHING HIM CAPTURE THE IMAGINATION OF FANS WORLDWIDE.

NAME: DAMIEN SANDOW
FROM: PALO ALTO, CALIFORNIA
YOU SHOULD KNOW: THIS SUPERSTAR SAYS HIS 'SOPHISTICATED IN-RING STYLE ELEVATES HIM ABOVE THOSE WHO WOULD DARE TO MUSTER A CHALLENGE'.

"And here come the champs! One of the most unlikely alliances in WWE history but The Big Red Monster and Daniel Bryan clearly work as team, they have the gold after all…"

"…Tonight's about payback for Team Hell No, both have taken beatings at the hands of Ziggler and Langston recently…"

"…how will things play out in a fair fight?"

"Are there no depths to which The Show Off won't sink! He's mocking Bryan's pre match kiss with AJ Lee from last year's *WrestleMania*. Daniel's not going to like this!"

"Bryan didn't like Ziggler's kiss one one bit! He's has torn into The Show Off quicker than he can shout 'Yes!'"

"Bryan's tossed him out of the ring. But there's no let up for The Show Off, Bryan has followed him out of the ring and thrown him back in.

"He's really making him pay for mocking him!"

"They're back in the ring and some how Ziggler has made the tag. This could be trouble for Bryan. Langston is 290 lbs of bad news!"

"Bryan didn't want any part of Big E, he's tagged in Kane!"

"This is real battle of strength v strength and Kane is going for the Choke Slam."

"Big E looks to have the measure of Team Hell No. Are we about to see the titles change hands?"

"But Langston has powered out of it and hit The Big Red Monster with a fearsome shot of his own!"

"And he catches Kane with an incredible drop kick! Wow, you could feel the hurt from here!"

"With Kane on his back Ziggler wants a piece of the action! The Ego isn't about to let his tag team partner get all the headlines"

"All Bryan can do is watch and hope the tag gets made so he can help his partner out…"

"Forget waiting, Bryan is taking matters into his own hands and scores a flying knee from the apron onto Langston. This match always looked like it could boil over and now it has. All hell has broken loose at *WrestleMania!*"

7 Which Superstar likes to lay out his opponents with a Backstabber?

8 Triple H's match against Brock Lesnar at *WrestleMania 29* was a No Holds Barred match, but what was the stipulation if The Game lost?

9 To the nearest 10 pounds – how much is the combined weight of Ryback and Mark Henry?

10 Which masked Superstar is taller, Rey Mysterio or Sin Cara?

11 Ted Dibiase has held the tag team title during his WWE career, what other title has been strapped around his waist?

12 Who famously fell in love with Aksana, causing its 'owner' all sorts of problems?

13 What match did John Cena win to earn his shot at The Rock and the WWE title at *WrestleMania 29*?

14 Fandango has refused to wrestle several WWE Superstars for the same reason since he arrived on the scene. Why did he turn the matches down?

NAME THAT: SIGNATURE MOVE

MOVE DESCRIPTION:

This huge Indian Superstar takes no chances when finishing his opponents. While his rival is dazed he slaps his enormous hand around their neck, lifts them high above his head, a full nine feet into the air before slamming them down on to their backs and covering them for the one, two, three.

MOVE DESCRIPTION:

Brit battler Wade utilises all his street fighting smarts to dispatch Superstars in the WWE ring. Barrett's technical move begins with an adapted cross-face. While they're trapped in his arms he grips their wrist and sends them spinning. As the embattled foe spins he uses their motion as a weapon against them and slams a vicious elbow into their jaw, putting them out for the count!

MOVE DESCRIPTION:

Technique and ring craft are all well and good but when the Dublin brawler wants to end a match he doesn't like to hang around! Quick and devastating, Sheamus simply smashes a raised boot into his opponent's face. Simple, but effective!

As well as having the best athletes in sports entertainment, the WWE also has the best finishers in the game! Each are in equal parts memorable and deadly, but can you name these Superstars' signature moves from a description alone? Take this quiz and find out.

MOVE DESCRIPTION:

Just as nasty as the man himself, The Miz has developed one of the most-effective finishing moves in WWE history. Brilliant in its simplicity, the end begins with an old school Half-Nelson hold. Wily Miz then sweeps his leg in front of his rivals and pulls a simple, playground trip. However, with Miz still holding the half-nelson, the stricken opponent lands face first.

MOVE DESCRIPTION:

So fast it's almost impossible to see what has happened! Truth's finisher is as dazzling as it is deadly. Truth sends his rival flying into the ropes before dashing in the other direction. When the pair meet in the centre of the ring, R-Truth uncorks an incredible spinning, flying forearm!

MOVE DESCRIPTION:

A deadly mixture of power and technique, this is one move no one gets up from! Ryback uses all his strength to pick his opponents up in a fireman's carry. But rather than carrying them to safety, he throws his feet into the air, driving his rival into the mat.

WRESTLE WITH THE DIFFERENCES

WrestleMania 29 featured some of the greatest matches ever to take place in the ring. Mark Henry and Ryback's barnstormer became an instant classic, sure to be discussed by fanatics for years to come. But how closely were you following the action? We've made 10 subtle differences to the picture on the right, can you find them all?

"Of course, threats and slurs weren't the only thing Swagger did in the build up to tonight's match. He also broke Ricardo Rodriguez's ankle.

"Del Rio lifts the title high. But tonight's not just about the gold for Del Rio, tonight he's after vengeance too!"

"I don't think we've ever seen the champ so focused!"

"Del Rio's eager to get things started. A quick reminder from the ref about what's on the line. And we're off!"

"It's a fast start from Alberto, he nails Swagger with vicious clothesline, you could hear that one in the refreshment stall outside the arena!"

"And he's not letting up as he lands a brutal back breaker on Swagger. ADR looks like a man possessed tonight."

"This could be a short night. Del Rio follows up side kick to the downed Swagger…"

"Alberto throws Jack into turnbuckle and is following him straight in… but Jack shows all of his experience and cunning and moves out of the way to send the champ smashing into ring post. It's game on!"

"Swagger keeps up the punishment with a body splash off the top rope. The tables have turned, it looks like there's only going to be one winner now."

"Swagger locks in cross face choke, he's making Del Rio pay for losing his focus.

"Somehow Del Rio finds the strength to reverse the pin and goes for the one, two, three. But Colter has dragged Jack's legs onto the rope, stopping the count."

"Rodriguez has spotted it and comes to Del Rio's aid. But with a broken ankle, how much help can he be? Oh no, Colter has attacked Ricardo and stolen his crutches!"

"Watch out Del Rio! The champ has turned his attention away from Swagger and rushed to his personal announcer's rescue."

"It was a ploy! Swagger makes a cowardly attack on the champ!"

"He's sneaked up behind him and is sending the champ face first into front row."

"Wow, Del Rio hit the stands like a ton of bricks. I think we're witnessing Del Rio's last moments as the champion. Surely there's no way back from the beating Swagger's putting on him!"

"And the action is back in the ring. Swagger's setting Del Rio up for the finish."

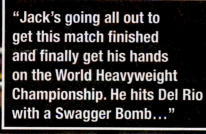

"Jack's going all out to get this match finished and finally get his hands on the World Heavyweight Championship. He hits Del Rio with a Swagger Bomb…"

"…now he's locking on Patriot Lock onto Del Rio's leg. He can't take much more of this…"

"Del Rio grabs the rope! The ref forces Swagger to release the hold. After the beating he's taken, where is Alberto finding the strength to continue?"

"Back comes the champ! It's amazing that Del Rio is even standing on that leg, let alone using it to land a high kick on Swagger's head. That's what they call Championship quality folks!"

"I can't believe it, Del Rio's locked in a Cross Armbreaker and Swagger taps out! What a turnaround for the champion!"

"When all looked lost he reached deep within himself and did what it took to keep his title!"

"Alberto can't believe it himself! It's an emotional night for the champ and Rodriguez!"

"He keeps the title and is now finally clear of the Swagger and Colter monkey that's lived on his back for the last few months!"

SUPERSTAR COLOUR MATCH

GET STUCK INTO THE ACTION OF *WRESTLEMANIA 29!*

CM Punk and Undertaker are battling it out! Grab your felt tip pens or pencils and add some colour to the action . . .

SWITCHED UP SUPERSTARS

Look at these terrifying Superstars! We've created two brand new 'ultimate Superstars' from the body parts of some of the WWE's finest. Can you work out whose frames we've 'borrowed' to make our ultimate combatants?

Write down your answers in the boxes below.

THE ULTIMATE HIGH FLYER

Head:

Torso:

Arms:

Legs:

THE POWERHOUSE

Head:

Upper Body:

Legs:

Boots:

THE BIG W QUIZ P2

They're some of the most recognizable faces on the planet, but have you been paying attention to the details? In the second part of the big quiz, see if you can work out the Superstar with just the slightest glimpse. Name the owners of these body parts.

1 This belongs to:

2 This belongs to:

3 This belongs to:

4 This belongs to:

5 This belongs to:

6 This belongs to:

TRIPLE H

VITAL STATISTICS: TRIPLE H

WHO: THE KING OF KINGS

HEIGHT: 6' 4"

WEIGHT: 255 LBS

FROM: GREENWICH, CONNECTICUT

SIGNATURE MOVE: PEDIGREE

YOU SHOULD KNOW:

The King of Kings, Triple H has gone from being a co-founder of D-Generation X to a mentor for future main eventers Randy Orton and Batista to a future Hall of Famer and high ranking executive at WWE headquarters. It's no joke to say Triple H hasn't just existed on the cutting edge, he's been the one sharpening the blade!

"Here we go folks. Hold onto your hats, this is going to be nasty. No holds are barred in this match-up."

"Is there a more fearsome Superstar in the WWE right now the Big Bad Brock Lesnar? 6' 3" and 226 lbs of fast, powerful and highly skilled bad intentions!"

"Lesnar's got a point to prove tonight and he's promised the fans he will stop at nothing to make sure he makes it!"

"The stakes couldn't be higher for the Game tonight. It's simple, lose the match tonight and he has to leave the WWE.

"He's fighting for survival, and not just in sports entertainment."

"But in a no-holds barred match against an opponent like Lesnar, he'll need every ounce of fight he has to make it through the night too!"

"But Triple H isn't completely on his own to deal with Brock. His good friend and Hall of Famer Shawn Michaels is here with him too. Can the Heartbreak Kid help the Game keep his job?"

"And the action is under way. Brock lands a heavy knee to Triple H's breadbasket and quickly attacks him by the ropes."

"The Game is playing possum! He dodges Lesnar and sends the action to the arena floor.

"Buckle in folks, this match could be a heck of a ride!"

"The Game's going for the cover. The crowd here at the Met Life Center count along. One, two, three!"

"And what a match-up. Broken, bloodied and scarred, The Game's run goes on!"

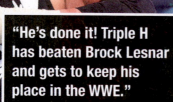

"He's done it! Triple H has beaten Brock Lesnar and gets to keep his place in the WWE."

"Triple H and Shawn Michaels go on to fight another day. What a display of intestinal fortitude from Triple H!"

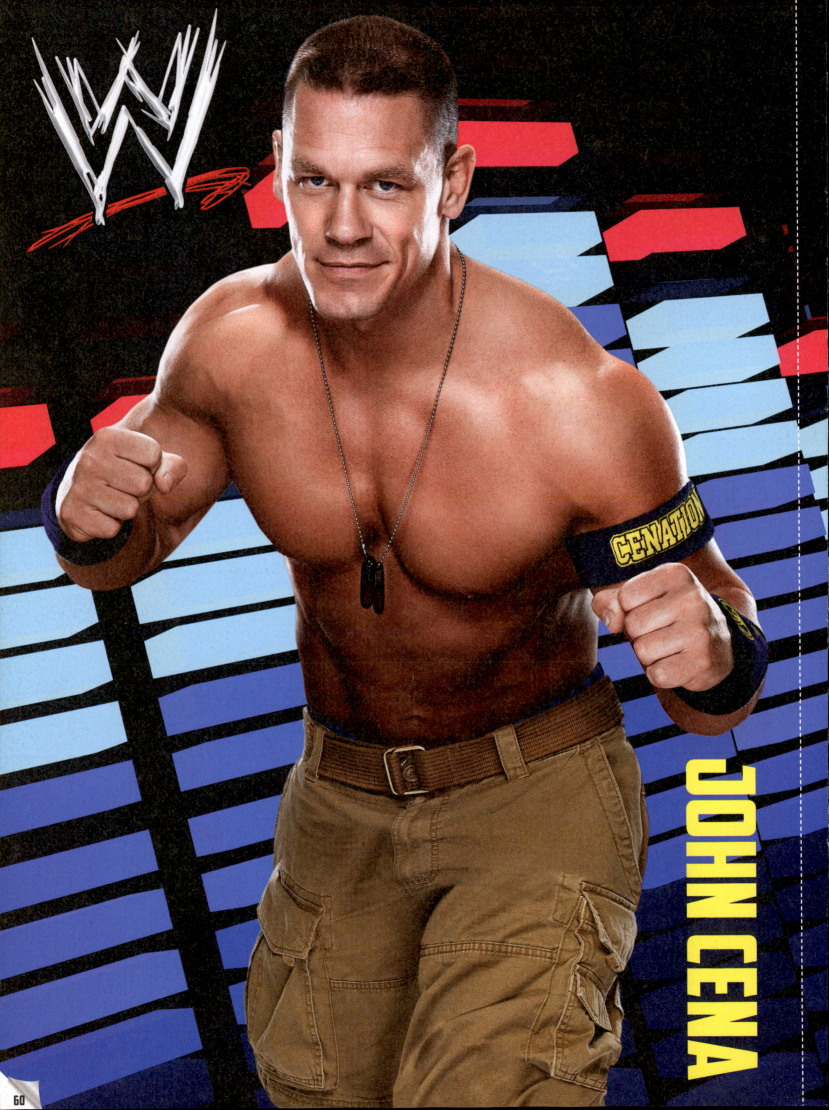

JOHN CENA

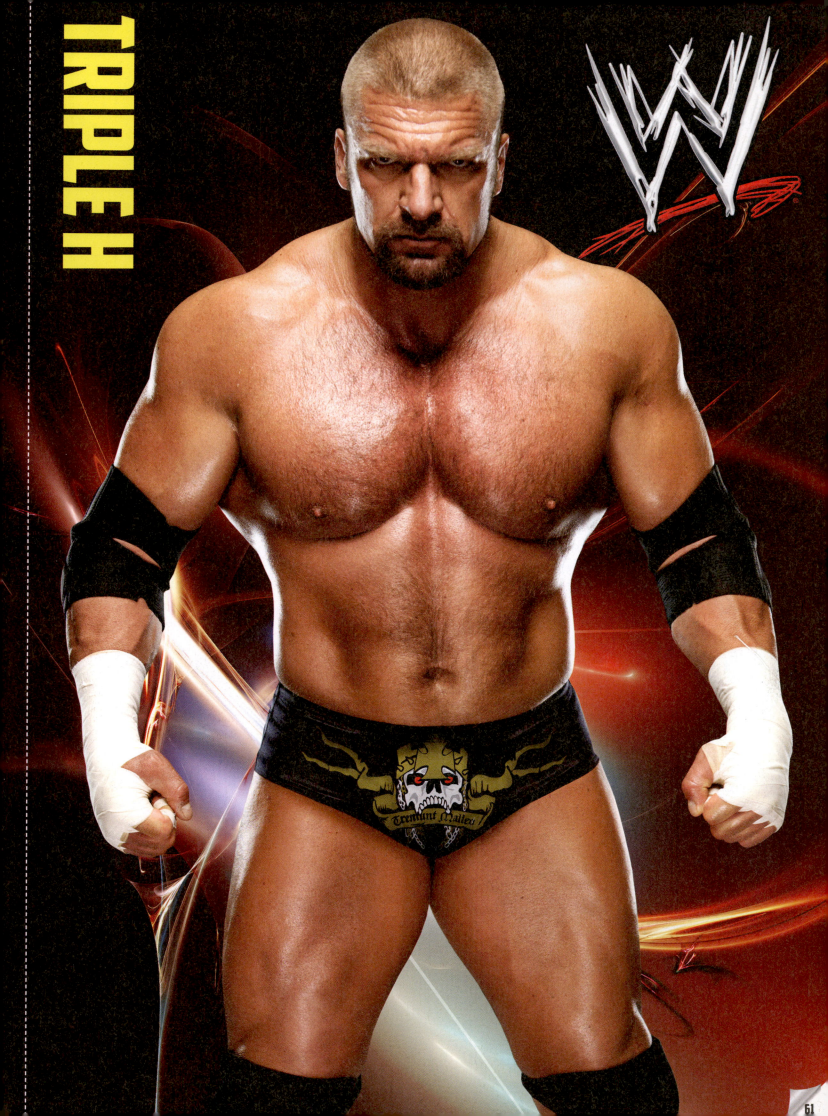

TRIPLE H

W

61

DIVAS ▶▶

NAME: KAITLYN
FROM: HOUSTON, TEXAS
YOU SHOULD KNOW: PRIOR TO HER WWE DEBUT, THIS BEAUTIFUL AND SPUNKY DIVA SPENT YEARS MAKING HER NAME IN COMPETITIVE FITNESS AND BODYBUILDING.

NAME: AJ LEE
FROM: UNION CITY, NEW JERSEY
YOU SHOULD KNOW: DON'T BE FOOLED BY AJ'S GIRLISH CHARMS. SHE'S A NEVER-SAY-DIE COMPETITOR AND AS DANGEROUS AS ANY DIVA IN THE WWE.

NAME: AKSANA
FROM: ALYTUS, LITHUANIA
YOU SHOULD KNOW: AKSANA HAS BEEN SPOTTED ON THE ARM OF SUPERSTARS ANTONIO CESARO AND TEDDY LONG. BUT DON'T MISTAKE HER FOR SIMPLY ARM CANDY.

NAME: LAYLA
FROM: LONDON, ENGLAND
YOU SHOULD KNOW: BEFORE FINDING FAME AND FORTUNE IN THE WWE, LONDON-BORN LAYLA WAS A DANCER FOR THE MIAMI HEAT BASKETBALL TEAM.

5. To increase the pain caused by one of his already-very-painful chops to the chest, Big Show removed Dean Ambrose's Shield vest during their match up.

YES! ☐ NO! ☐

6. Fandango's *WrestleMania* match with Chris Jericho was actually the first time he'd fought in a WWE ring.

YES! ☐ NO! ☐

7. During one attack, Brock Lesnar added insult to Triple H by performing a Pedigree, Triple H's own finishing move, on him.

YES! ☐ NO! ☐

8. Paul Heyman was in the corner of three Superstars during the *WrestleMania* event.

YES! ☐ NO! ☐

9. During his match with John Cena, The Rock was hit with no less than four Attitude Adjustments.

YES! ☐ NO! ☐

10. Dolph Ziggler tried to use his *Money In The Bank* briefcase as a weapon against Kane in their tag match.

YES! ☐ NO! ☐

CM PUNK

VITAL STATISTICS: CM PUNK

HEIGHT:	6' 2"
WEIGHT:	218 LBS
FROM:	CHICAGO, ILLINOIS
SIGNATURE MOVE:	GO TO SLEEP, ANACONDA VICE

YOU SHOULD KNOW:

Tattoos, body-piercings, everything about CM Punk is anti-establishment hell-raiser. It's no surprise then to learn that his biggest inspiration is Hall-of-famer Rowdy Roddy Piper, another Superstar who liked nothing better than 'sticking it to the man'.

UNDERTAKER

VITAL STATISTICS: UNDERTAKER

HEIGHT: 6' 10"

WEIGHT: 299 LBS

FROM: DEATH VALLEY

SIGNATURE MOVE: TOMBSTONE, CHOKESLAM, LAST RIDE

YOU SHOULD KNOW:

No one in all of sports entertainment has a *WrestleMania* to match the Undertaker. Heading into his match against Punk he boasted a 20-0 record, but did he keep his winning streak going?

"Here he is folks, the self-proclaimed Best in the World, CM Punk."

"He's going to need to be more than the best tonight though."

"And as if the stakes weren't high enough already, Paul Heyman has brought 'Taker's own urn to the ring with him!"

"In facing Undertaker at *WrestleMania*, Punk faces a challenge no one has yet found an answer to, will he be able to find the answer no Superstar has found yet?"

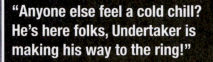

"Anyone else feel a cold chill? He's here folks, Undertaker is making his way to the ring!"

"He's on a record-breaking 20-0 win streak at *WrestleMania*, is there anything more scary than facing the Dead Man at this event?"

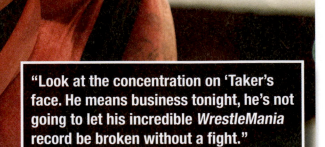

"Look at the concentration on 'Taker's face. He means business tonight, he's not going to let his incredible *WrestleMania* record be broken without a fight."

"Punk looks ready though, it'll be interesting to see what his game plan for victory is tonight. If there's anyone in the WWE with the skills and experience to get this job done, it's CM Punk."

"Uh oh – this isn't the start Punk wanted though! Undertaker has got his hands on him almost immediately and slams him into the turnbuckle."

"Wait a minute, this could be over quickly. The Dead Man hoists Punk into the air for a Chokeslam!

"CM is canny though, he breaks out of the hold and is now launching his own high kick attack!"

"It's going to take more than a high kick to beat Underaker at *WrestleMania* though and soon the Dead Man is back in control of the match. He scores with a vicious high boot of his own!"

"He must be five feet in the air! Undertaker lands a devastating leg drop."

"There's no let up for Punk! The Dead Man has a hold of his hand and looks to be setting up his trademark walk along the top rope."

"But Punk's not ready to roll over yet. He yanks Undertaker's arm and sends his rival smashing into the ring."

"Now it's time for CM Punk to start landing his own offensive shots. He's mocking Undertaker! He's climbed the top rope and is going to use The Dead Man's trademark moves on him!"

"He locks in a tight neck crank and you can see the pain on Undertaker. This will sap the big man's energy in a hurry."

"Time for Punk to start using some of the moves that he claims make him the best in the world. First he scores with a devastating high cross body…"

"…now he's tied Undertaker up and snaps him back to the canvas with a nasty, painful neck breaker…"

"…Punk is scaling the ropes again, this time to drop a colossal elbow drop. He goes for the cover, but rather than using his usual technique to get the three-count, Punk is poking more fun at the Undertaker by mimicking his trademark pin style. This is dangerous territory from CM Punk!"

"The action switches to the outside of the ring. CM Punk is determined to win this match, he's climbed up the corner post again…"

"…and this time hits Undertaker with an enormous flying elbow from the top rope. I think they heard that one back in Death Valley!"

"But what is Punk doing? Rather than keeping up the momentum, he's stopped to poke fun at the Dead Man again…"

"…and gets caught in a textbook Tombstone! Can you believe this? CM Punk had victory within his grasp and he's thrown the opportunity away to instead tease the future hall of famer."

"One, two, three! Oh the inhumanity! He's done it, Undertaker has beaten CM Punk!"

"And he's extended his *WrestleMania* record to an incredible 21-0! Surely, that will never be bettered?!"

"Tonight we witnessed history folks! Undertaker leaves the Met Life Arena with the win, his amazing *WrestleMania* record intact and gets his famous urn back!"

THE BIG W QUIZ P3

We've checked your general knowledge and put your observational skills to the test, so what's left to check in this final part of the quiz? WWE Superstars, in addition to their incredible in-ring skills, are masters of the mic – their interviews are sometimes as entertaining as their matches! Have you've been listening? See if you can work out who uttered these classic catchphrases.

1 WOO WOO WOO – YOU KNOW IT!

Who says it:

2 EXCUSE ME!

Who says it:

3 YES! YES! YES!

Who says it:

4 STRAIGHT EDGE MEANS I'M BETTER THAN YOU!

Who says it:

5 BOOM BOOM BOOM!

Who says it:

6 I AM A WRESTLING GOD!

Who says it:

THE ROCK

VITAL STATISTICS: THE ROCK

WHO: DWAYNE "THE ROCK" JOHNSON, THIRD-GENERATION STAR AND LEADER OF "TEAM BRING IT"

HEIGHT: 6' 5"

WEIGHT: 260 LBS

FROM: MIAMI, FLORIDA

SIGNATURE MOVE: ROCK BOTTOM, PEOPLE'S ELBOW

YOU SHOULD KNOW:

The Great One, The People's Champion and The Most Electrifying Man in All of Entertainment, and that's just what he calls himself! Fortunately for Rock, he has the charisma and toughness to back up every word!